sau•ro•pod

noun

A really big* plant-eating dinosaur, with a long neck*, and a long tail*, that stood on four legs*.

mostly - some were really, really big, and some were surprisingly small.

**again, *mostly*

***... *look*, just read the book, okay?

REXTOOTH STUDIOS

THE LARGEST ANIMALS TO EVER WALK THE EARTH

WRITTEN BY **TED RECHLIN** AND **CARY WOODRUFF**

EDITED BY **ANNE RECHLIN**

COPYRIGHT © 2021 BY TED RECHLIN AND CARY WODDRUFF

PUBLISHED BY REXTOOTH STUDIOS, BOZEMAN, MONTANA

ISBN: 978-1-7371242-0-7

ALL RIGHTS RESERVED. NO PART OF THIS BOOK MAY BE REPRODUCED IN WHOLE OR IN PART BY ANY MEANS IN ANY FORM WITHOUT PRIOR PERMISSION OF THE PUBLISHER, EXCEPT FOR BRIEF EXCERPTS FOR REVIEWS.

COVER DESIGN BY TED RECHLIN

PART ONE

GENESIS

In which a new creature steps into the spotlight, but stage fright is far from their most pressing concern...

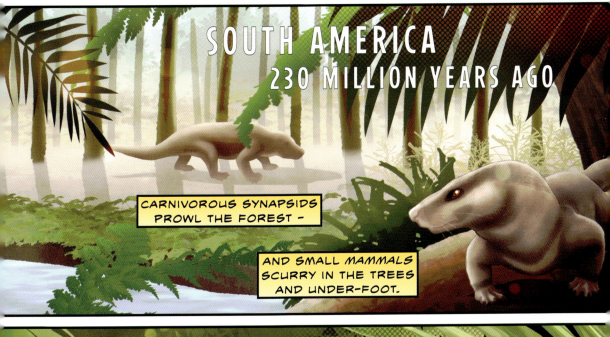

SOUTH AMERICA
230 MILLION YEARS AGO

CARNIVOROUS SYNAPSIDS PROWL THE FOREST—

AND SMALL MAMMALS SCURRY IN THE TREES AND UNDER-FOOT.

BUT THEY *ARE* HERE.

THESE DINOSAURS ARE CALLED **SATURNALIA**

AND THEY ARE FORE-RUNNERS TO *TITANS*.

WHEN YOU THINK 'SAUROPOD', YOU PROBABLY THINK *BIG*.

WELL... SATURNALIA'S *NOT*.

ABOUT THE SIZE OF THE FAMILY DOG, SIZE ISN'T EVEN THE MOST *PARADOXICAL* PART OF THIS CRITTER'S LINEAGE.

YOU'D BE FORGIVEN IF YOU THOUGHT SATURNALIA WAS THE ANCESTOR OF T. REX –

NOT BRACHIOSAURUS.

BUT *EVOLUTION* IS FUNNY LIKE THAT.

RUN.

THE LITTLE SAUROPODOMORPHS ARE EASY PREY.

GNATHOVORAX
- A HERRERASAURID PREDATOR.

IT'S NOT QUITE A THEROPOD DINOSAUR - AS FAR AS *PHYLOGENY* IS CONCERNED -

BUT THE SHARP *TEETH* AND BIG *CLAWS* ARE CLOSE ENOUGH THAT THE BEST STRATEGY FOR THE SATURNALIA IS -

BUT, THE GNATHOVORAX DOESN'T *REALIZE* -

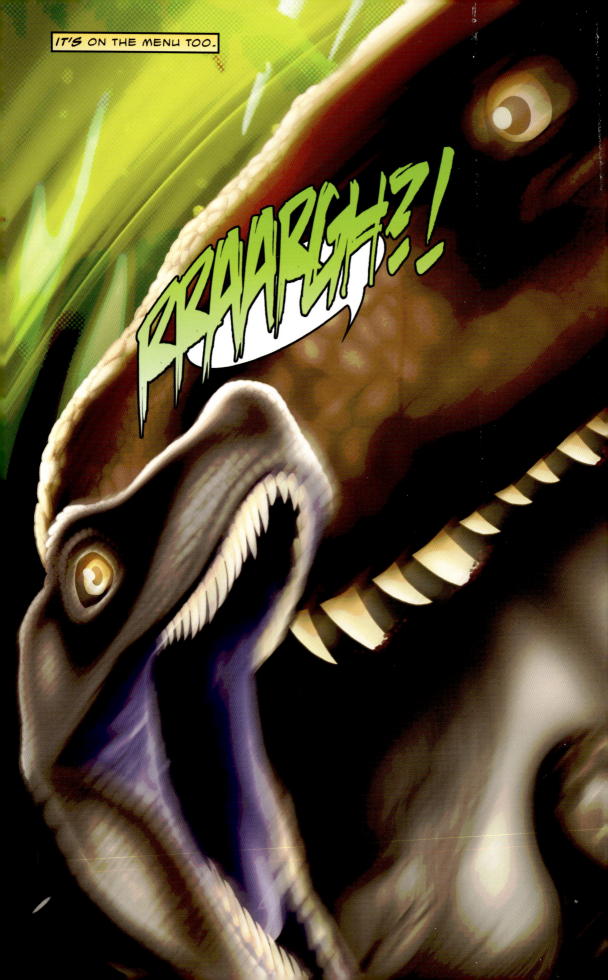

PART TWO

LEVEL-UP

In which the ancient 'pod ancestors embiggen, and face a new enemy...

ANTARCTICA
189 MILLION YEARS AGO

BUT IT WAS ONCE A *MUCH* DIFFERENT PLACE.

ANTARCTICA
PRESENT DAY

THE *SOUTH POLE* MAY NOT BE A PLACE THAT SCREAMS, '*DINOSAUR*' TO YOU – WITH ITS ICE CAPS AND SUB-ZERO TEMPERATURES –

SIDE-NOTE: THE SOUTH POLE IS *ACTUALLY* PRIME DINO-SAUR HABITAT TODAY – *MILLIONS* OF *PENGUINS* LIVE THERE QUITE HAPPILY.

SIDE-SIDE-NOTE: THESE ARE *PTEROSAURS* – A KIND OF *FLYING REPTILE* – NOT DINOSAURS.

THOUGH PERHAPS NOT BIG BY **TRUE SAUROPOD** STANDARDS –

AT 20 FEET LONG, AND 1,500 POUNDS, GLACIALISAURUS CERTAINLY DWARFS THE FAMILY DOG.

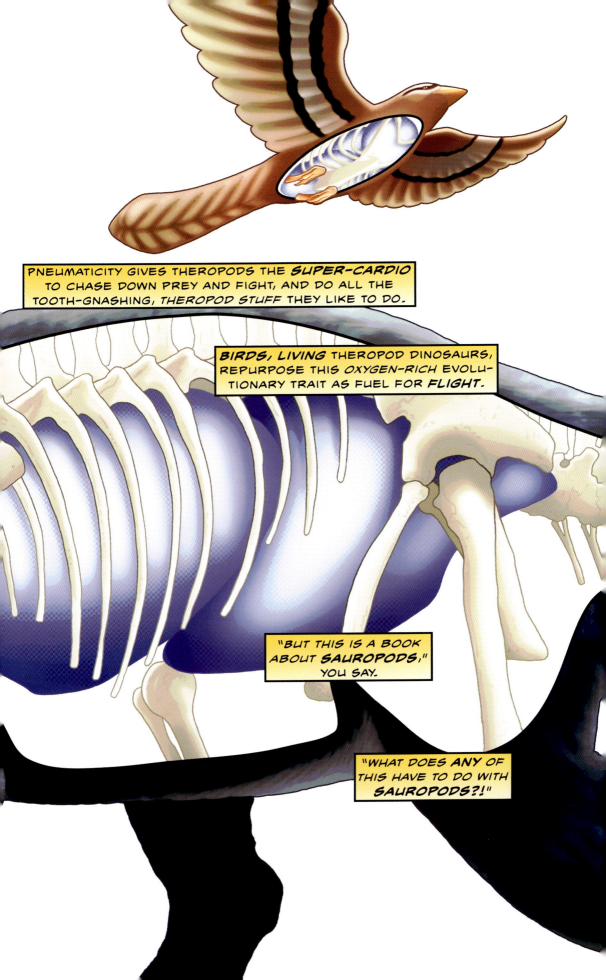

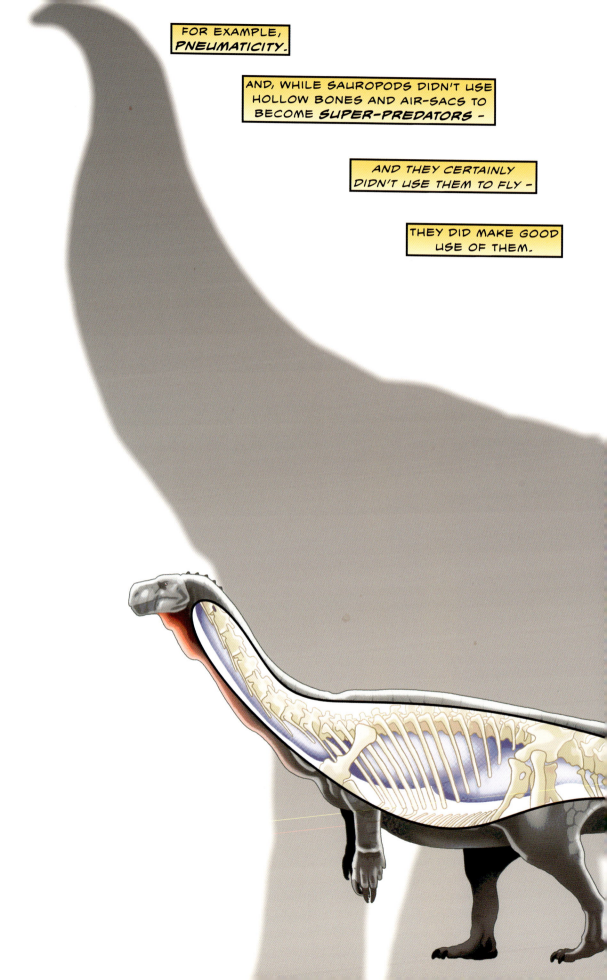

THE QUESTION OF *WHY* THE SAUROPODS GREW SO LARGE IS A HARD ONE TO ANSWER.

ECOLOGICAL CHANGES MAY HAVE LED THEM TO UTILIZE DIFFERENT FOOD SOURCES.

AN *EVER-EXPANDING* GUT MAY HAVE *FORCED* THEM ONTO FOUR LEGS.

BUT ONE THING IS FOR *SURE*.

THEY *NEVER* COULD HAVE ATTAINED SUCH TREMENDOUS SIZES WITHOUT *LIGHTENING* THE LOAD.

NOT TO MENTION THAT ALL THAT EXTRA AIR WOULD BE A *BIG* HELP TO A *BIG* ANIMAL THAT WANTED TO... WELL... *BREATHE*.

SO HOLLOW BONES AND AIR-SACS WERE *JUST THE TICKET*.

PART THREE

THUNDER LIZARDS

In which all your favorites show up...

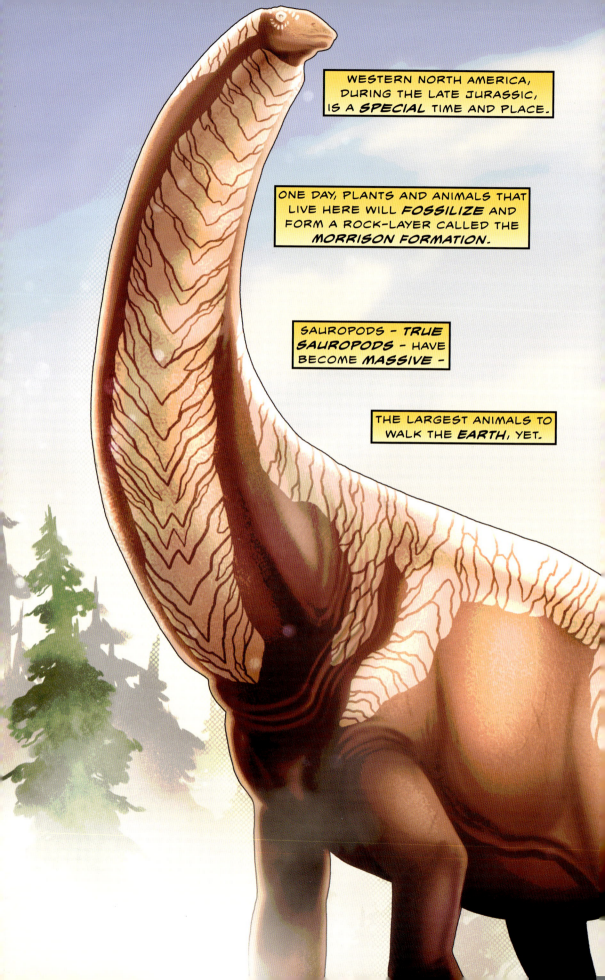

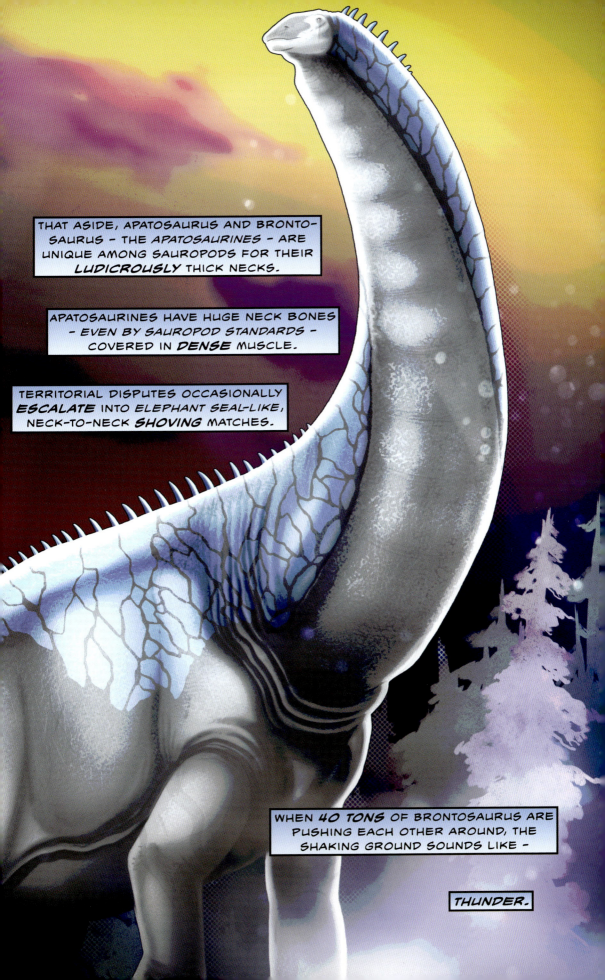

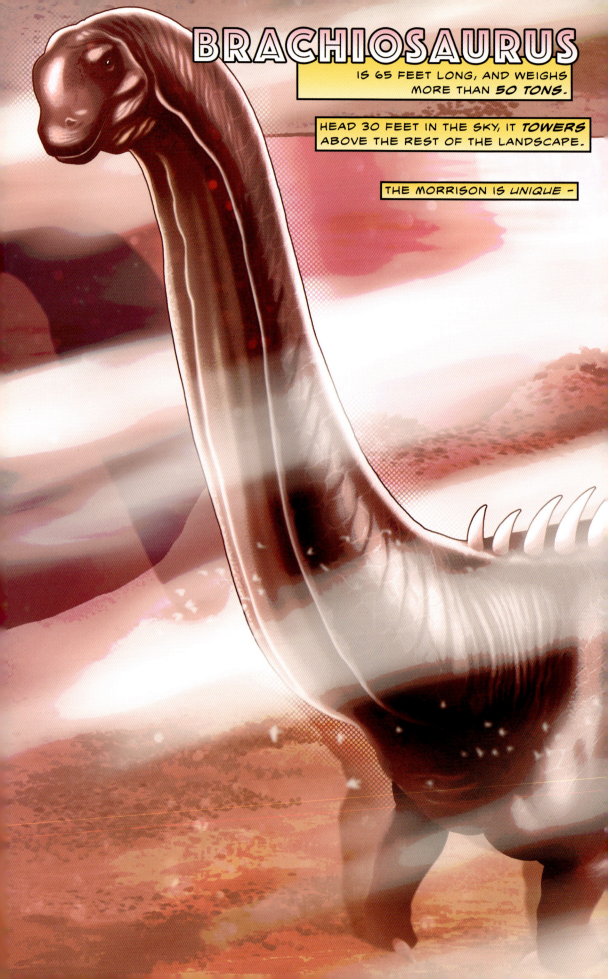

ITS GOT A WHOLE **BUNCH** OF SAUROPOD DINOSAURS –

ALL **GIANT** HERBIVORES, WHO NEED TO EAT ALMOST **ALL THE TIME** –

ALL LIVING IN THE **SAME** PLACE.

THIS SHOULD BE **IMPOSSIBLE**, OR AT LEAST **UNTENABLE**.

BUT EVOLUTION HAS CRAFTED A **WORK-AROUND** TO THIS PROBLEM.

CAMARASAURUS HAS TEETH SUITED FOR REALLY **TOUGH** PLANTS.

THE APATOSAURINES PREFER SOFTER FARE, FERNS AND THE LIKE.

BRACHIOSAURUS IS A **HIGH-BROWSER**.

THIS IS CALLED **NICHE-PARTITIONING**.

BASICALLY, THEY ALL STAY OUT OF EACH OTHER'S **WAY**.

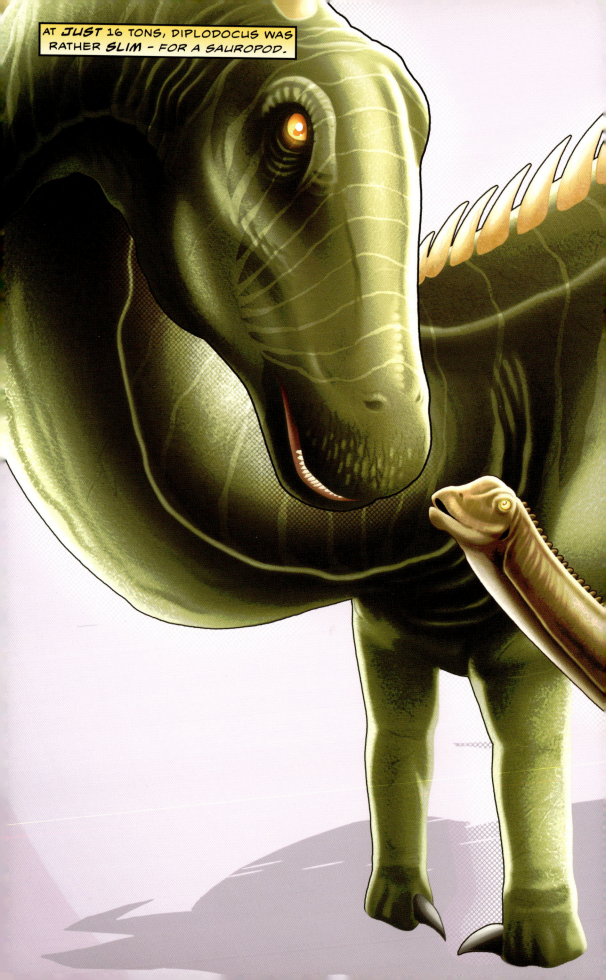

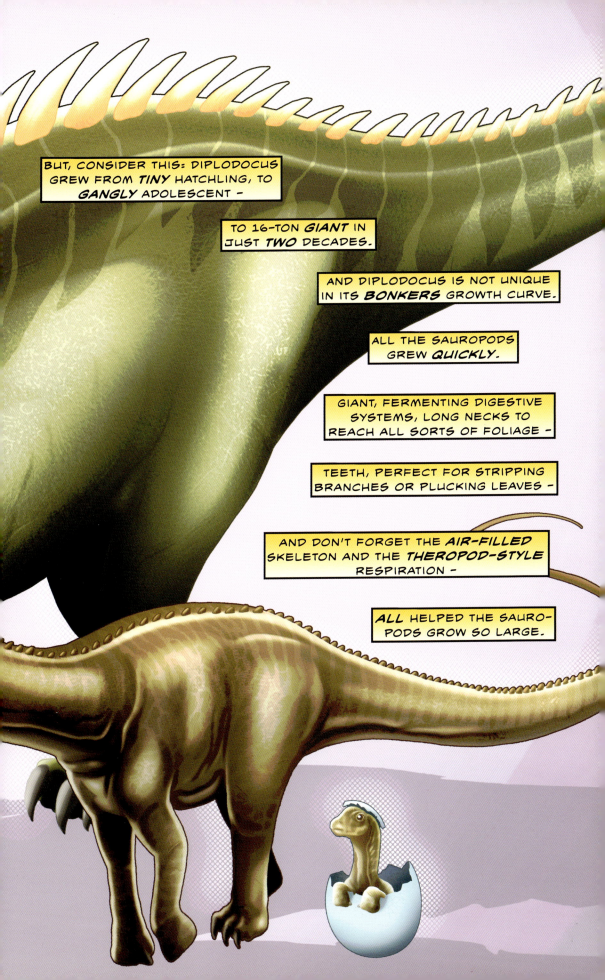

THE CARNIVORES OF THE LATE JURASSIC ARE LARGE AND *FEROCIOUS*.

THIS CERATOSAURUS HAS HIS EYES ON THE MUCH *EASIER* PRIZE —

FORTUNATELY —

HE DOESN'T HAVE TO.

THEY WERE ALSO *WEIRD*.

REALLY WEIRD.

THERE WERE *SPIKED* SAUROPODS, LIKE AMARGASAURUS & BAJADASAURUS WHO LOOK LIKE THEY BELONG AT A *HEAVY METAL* CONCERT —

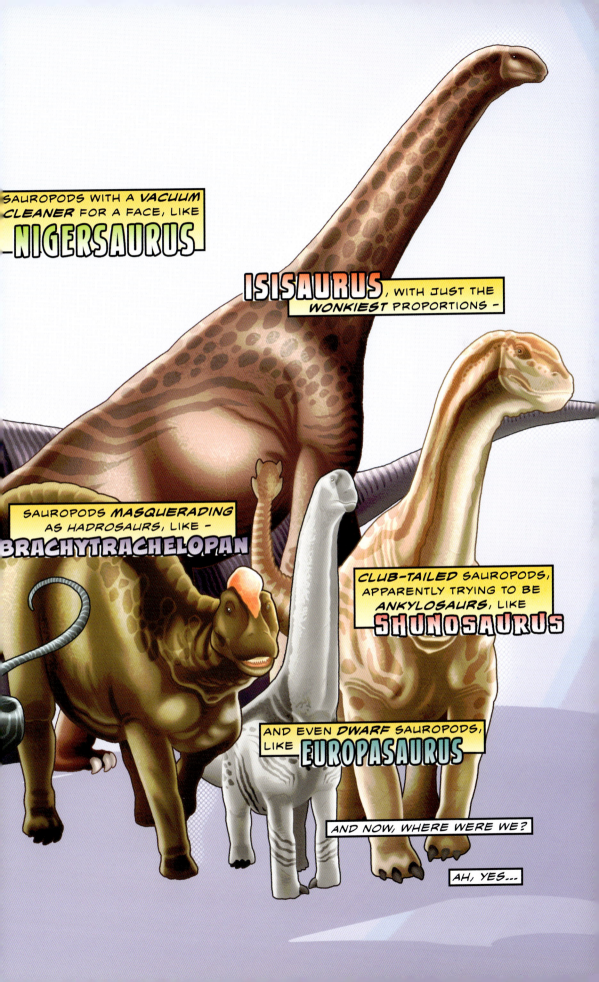

PART FOUR

THE TITANS

In which the dial goes up to eleven.

THEY WERE **MONUMENTAL MONSTERS** –

BEHEMOTHIC BEASTS –

GARGANTUAN GIANTS...

... LOOK, ONE REALLY RUNS OUT OF **SUPERLATIVES** TO DESCRIBE THEM.

TAKE FOR EXAMPLE,

PATAGOTITAN

DISCOVERED IN **PATAGONIA**, PATAGOTITAN STRETCHED TO **120 FEET LONG**, AND WEIGHED **70 TONS** –

AT LEAST, THAT'S HOW BIG WE KNOW THE **TYPE** SPECIMEN TO BE.

THE TYPE SPECIMEN, BY THE WAY, THAT WAS ONLY A **YOUNG** ADULT –

PERHAPS NOT **YET** FULLY-GROWN...

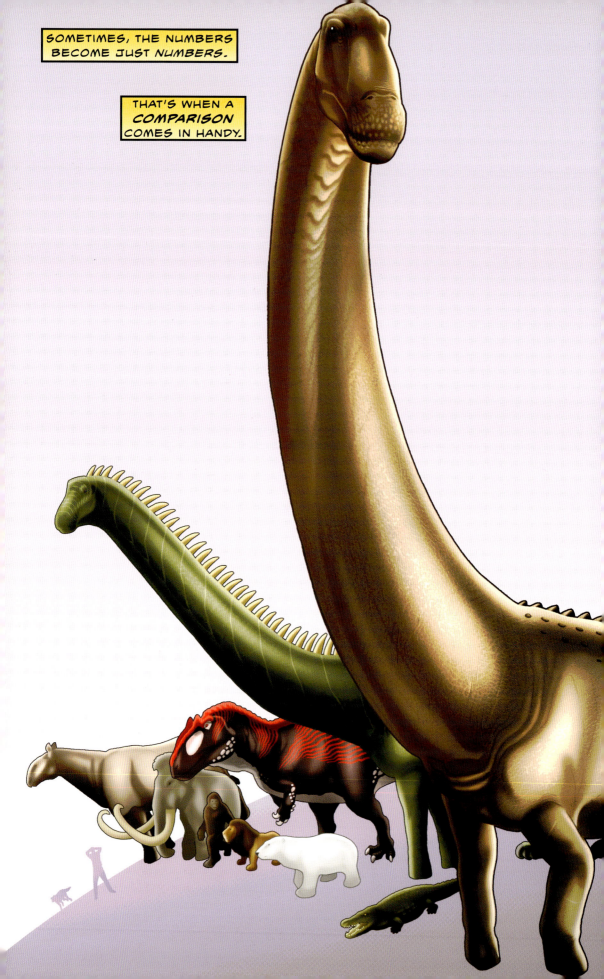

PATAGOTITAN, AND THE OTHER LARGE TITANOSAURS, **ABSOLUTELY** DWARF JUST ABOUT ANY OTHER ANIMAL YOU MIGHT THINK OF AS '*BIG*.'

THAT IS, OF COURSE, WITH A *NOTABLE* EXCEPTION...

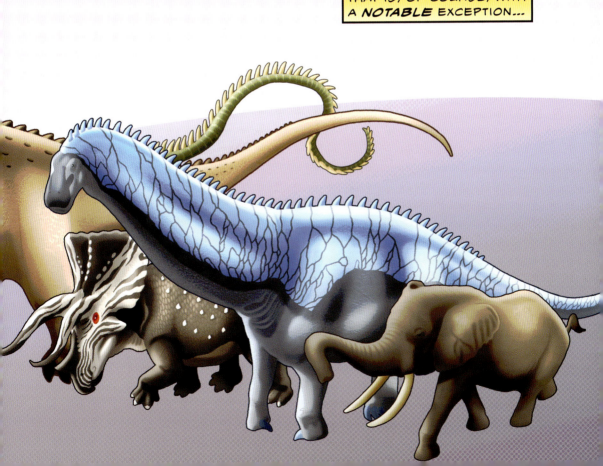

PATAGOTITAN AND ITS ILK WERE THE LARGEST ANIMALS TO EVER *WALK* THE EARTH...

BUT EVEN *THEY* ARE WELL OUT-SIZED BY THE **BLUE WHALE** — THE MOST *MASSIVE ANIMAL* TO EVER *LIVE* ON EARTH.

IN FACT, IN TERMS OF SHEER MASS, THE NEARLY *200-TON* BLUE WHALE IS MORE THAN *DOUBLE* THE WEIGHT OF THE LARGEST SAUROPOD.

BUT *NEITHER* ONE CAN LAY CLAIM TO THE TITLE OF LARGEST LIVING ORGANISM.

THE *GIANT SEQUOIA* TREE — ALSO KNOWN AS THE GIANT *REDWOOD* — CAN REACH MORE THAN *270* FEET TALL —

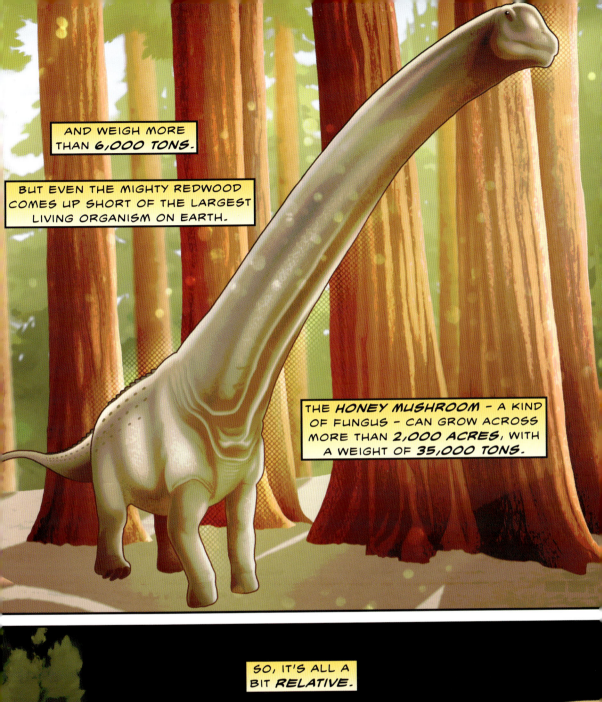

AND WEIGH MORE THAN 6,000 TONS.

BUT EVEN THE MIGHTY REDWOOD COMES UP SHORT OF THE LARGEST LIVING ORGANISM ON EARTH.

THE HONEY MUSHROOM — A KIND OF FUNGUS — CAN GROW ACROSS MORE THAN 2,000 ACRES, WITH A WEIGHT OF 35,000 TONS.

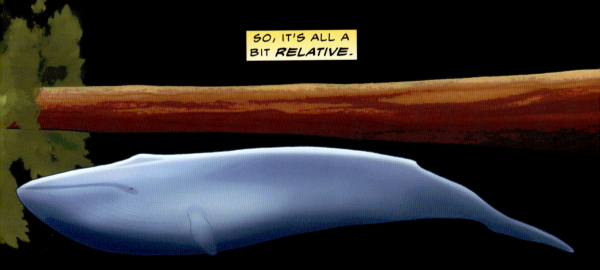

SO, IT'S ALL A BIT RELATIVE.

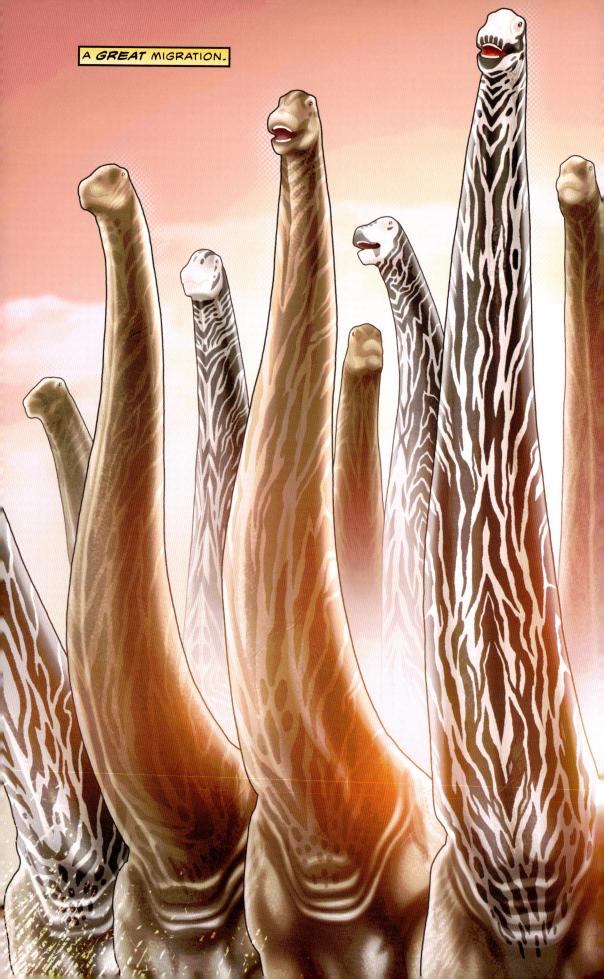

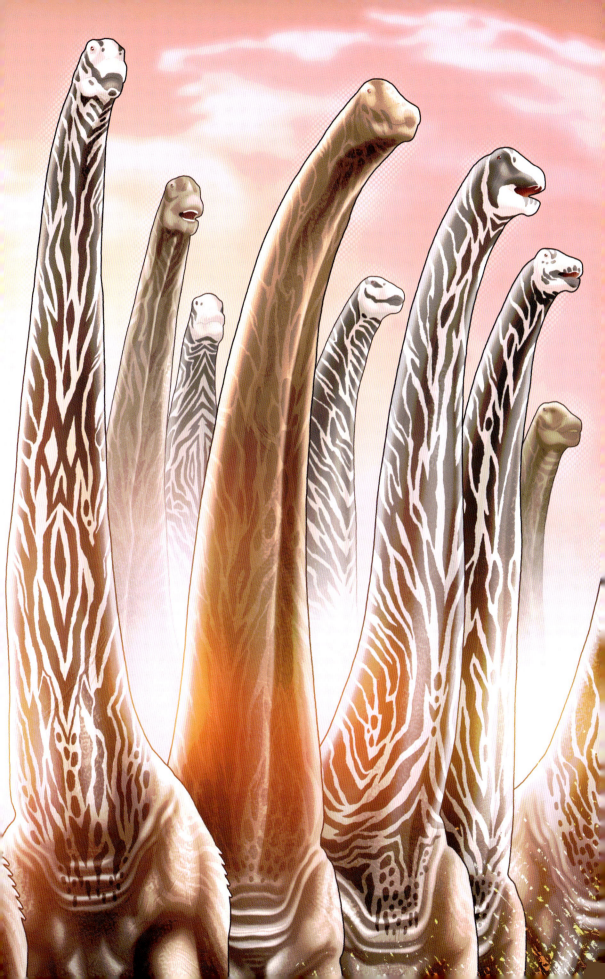

ALAMOSAURUS
– A TITANOSAUR – IS AMONG THE *LAST* OF THE SAUROPODS.

THE LARGE ADULTS IN THE HERD ARE OVER **90 FEET LONG**, AND WEIGH MORE THAN **60 TONS**.

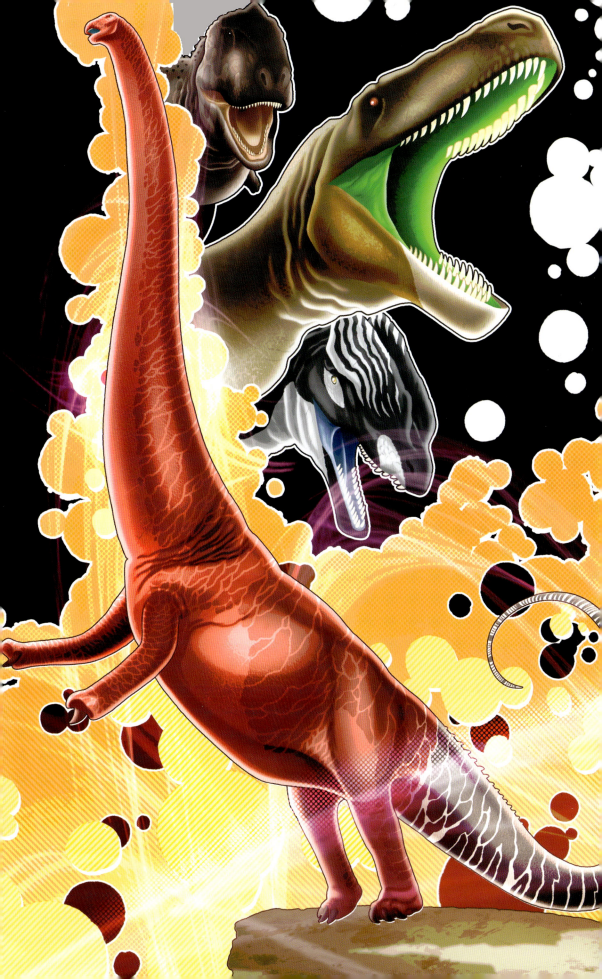

EVEN *ONE* HEALTHY, ADULT ALAMOSAURUS WOULD GIVE THEM A WORLD OF *TROUBLE*.

THAT'S WHY THEY'RE NOT AFTER A *HEALTHY*, ADULT ALAMOSAURUS.

THE ALAMOSAURUS MIGRATION IS A LONG ONE — COMING ALL THE WAY UP FROM SOUTHERN *NEW MEXICO*.

AND EVERY YEAR, THAT JOURNEY TAKES A *TOLL* ON THE HERD.

THE OLD, THE SICK, THEY HAVE A HARD TIME MAKING IT.

THEY'RE A *PERFECT* TARGET FOR A PACK OF HUNGRY T. REX.

UGH.

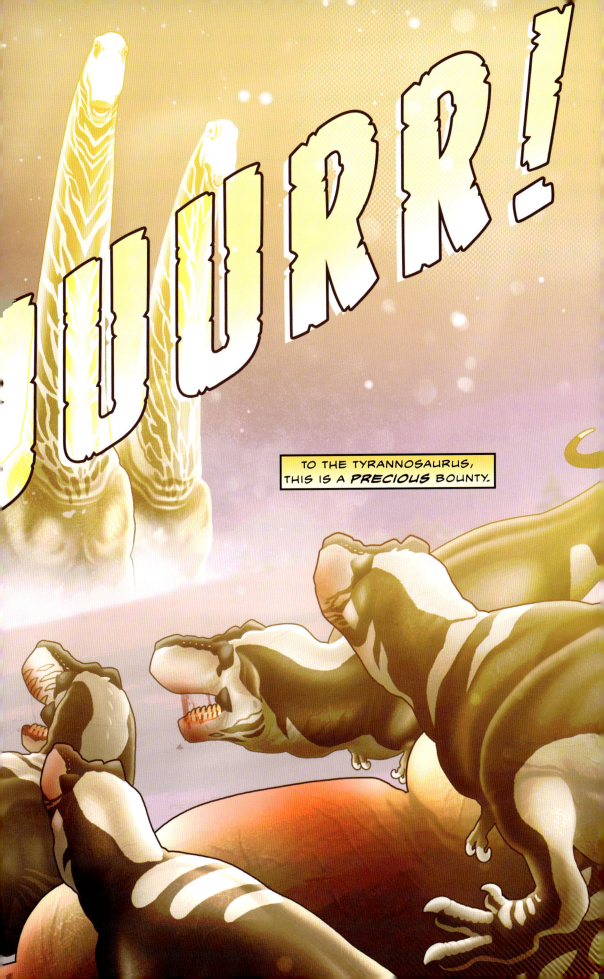

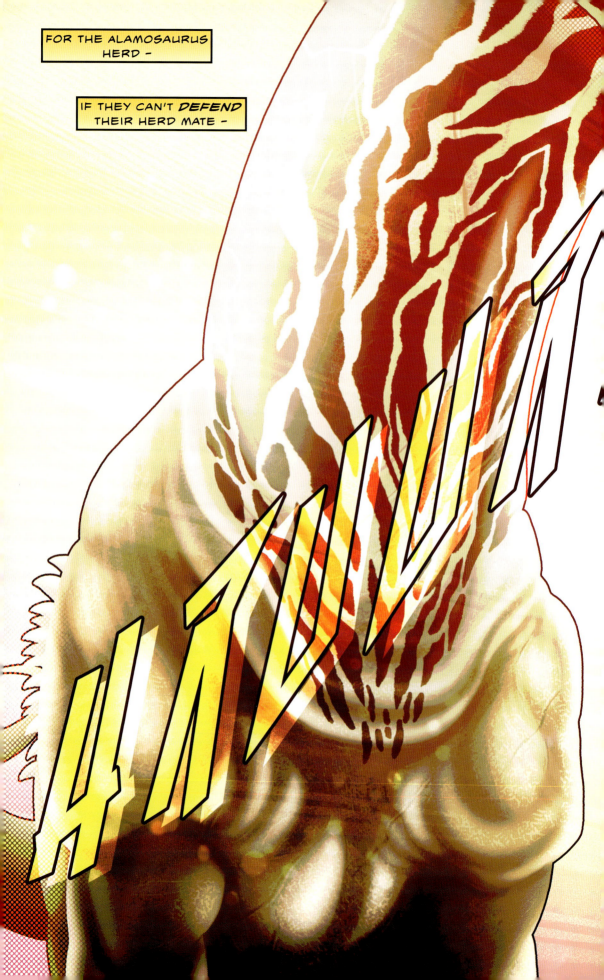

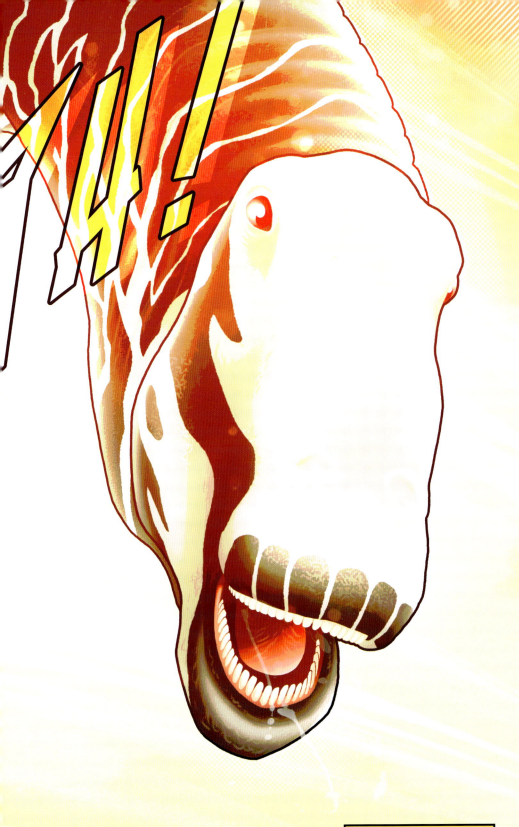

BUT THIS BRAWL OF THE WILD—

IS ABOUT TO BE CUT SHORT.

SIXTY-SIX MILLION YEARS AGO, A ROCK, THE SIZE OF *MOUNT EVEREST* SLAMMED INTO THE GULF OF MEXICO.

AND THE REIGN OF THE *NON-AVIAN* DINOSAURS CAME TO AN *END*.

IN THE TIME SINCE, MAMMALS ROSE UP TO DOMINATE THE GLOBE.

SOME OF THEM EVEN GREW QUITE LARGE.

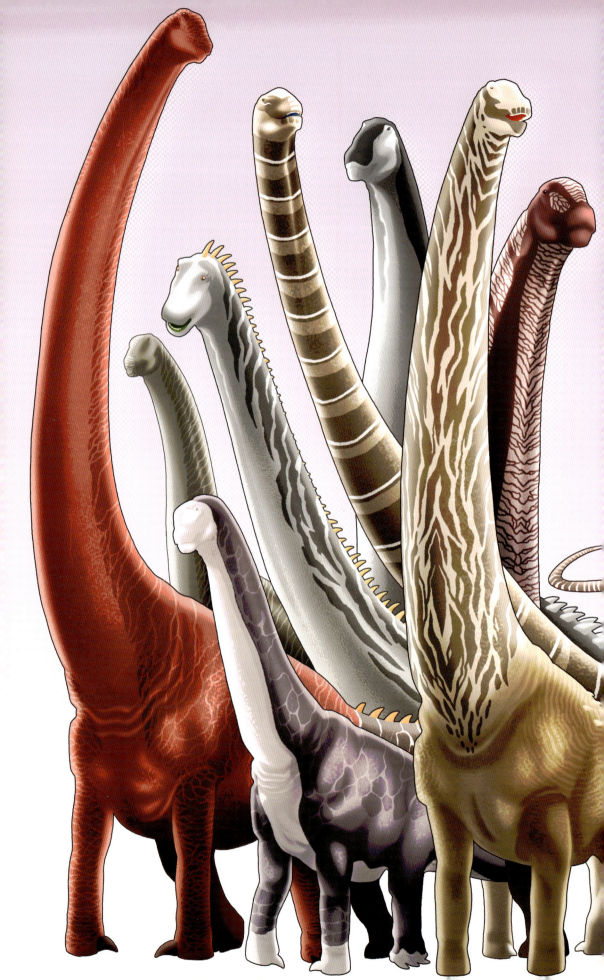

One reason for the popularity of dinosaurs is that they were the real **MONSTERS**. These gigantic beasts stalked the prehistoric earth, and unlike the imaginary childhood monster under your bed, for dinosaurs, we have **PROOF**. Go into a museum and you'll see the fossilized bones of these **MONSTERS**.

Sauropods didn't have the frills, crests, spikes, horns, claws, clubs, or teeth of many of the other famous dinosaurs. Instead, they wow us with their size. It's not **ONLY** that sauropods were big that fascinates us, but also **HOW** they got to be so big. Imagine you're holding an egg with a baby **DIPLODOCUS** inside. That egg is about the size of a cantaloupe. Soon after hatching, that baby Diplodocus is 6 feet long. By the age of 15, it's already **60 FEET LONG**, and as an adult at the age of 30, that Diplodocus is over **80 FEET LONG**. The sauropods were the biggest animals to ever walk the earth, and they didn't even come from the largest eggs. Sauropods are proof that great things start from humble beginnings.

It's not just about understanding how **FAST** they grew, there are so many more questions that **NEED** to be asked! How do you breathe with a **40-FOOT** windpipe and not **PASS OUT** between breaths? How much food did the **BIGGEST** animal to ever walk the earth need to **EAT** each day? If you could put one in a zoo, how big could it get, and how long could it live? At what age did they start laying eggs? How did males and females tell each other apart? How did they **COMMUNICATE**? What kinds of sounds could they make? Did they have good eyesight or other senses? How many **TITANS** could an ecosystem support?

It's all of these questions, and more, that together make the mystery of the **SAUROPOD**.

There are many **AMAZING** paleontologists today that are trying to answer these questions and solve these sauropod mysteries. But we won't solve them all. It's up to **YOU**, and the **NEXT GENERATIONS** of paleontologists to pick up where we leave off. Together, we'll understand all of the amazing extinct creatures of earth's past better than we could **EVER** imagine.

- Dr. Cary Woodruff,
  Paleontologist, Museum Curator, Educator, Author,
  CHAMPION OF SAUROPODS

REXTOOTH STUDIOS
REXTOOTH.COM

THE EARTH IS FOUR AND A HALF BILLION YEARS OLD.

COMPLEX LIFE DEVELOPED FIVE HUNDRED AND EIGHTY MILLION YEARS AGO.

IN THAT TIME OUR PLANET HAS BEEN HOME TO SOME TRULY AMAZING ANIMALS AND HAS BEEN THE STAGE FOR INCREDIBLE DRAMAS AND ADVENTURES.

REXTOOTH STUDIOS IS A PUBLISHER TELLING STORIES ABOUT THE AWESOME CREATURES THAT HAVE CALLED - AND STILL DO CALL - OUR PLANET HOME.

THE BOTTOM LINE IS REXTOOTH PRODUCES COOL STORIES WITH A FOCUS ON SCIENCE EDUCATION. THE MISSION STATEMENT IS AS SIMPLE AS THAT.

MORE BOOKS FROM REXTOOTH STUDIOS

LOOK FOR THESE TITLES AT YOUR LOCAL STORE, ONLINE, OR AT REXTOOTH.COM

ABOUT THE AUTHORS

AUTHOR AND ILLUSTRATOR TED RECHLIN HAS BEEN DRAWING PICTURES AND TELLING STORIES SINCE HE WAS TWO YEARS OLD. WHILE HIS DRAWING STYLE HAS EVOLVED, HIS STORIES HAVEN'T REALLY CHANGED MUCH. THEY'RE STILL ABOUT SCIENCE, NATURE, AND LOTS (AND LOTS) OF DINOSAURS. TED FOUNDED REXTOOTH STUDIOS SO HE COULD SHARE HIS PASSION FOR ALL THINGS NATURAL HISTORY AND SCIENCE EDUCATION.

CARY GREW UP IN THE FARM COUNTRY OF VIRGINIA, AND RECEIVED HIS B.SC. AND M.SC. IN EARTH SCIENCES AT MONTANA STATE UNIVERSITY UNDER DR. JACK HORNER, AND HIS PH.D AT THE UNIVERSITY OF TORONTO WORKING WITH DR. DAVID EVANS. CARY HAS PUBLISHED SEVERAL SCIENTIFIC PAPERS AND CHILDRENS BOOKS, AND HIS RESEARCH INTERESTS RANGE FROM THE VERY FIRST BURROWING DINOSAUR EVER DISCOVERED, STEGOSAURS, TAPHONOMY (WHAT HAPPENS FROM DEATH TO DISCOVERY), PACHYCEPHALOSAURS, FOSSIL DISEASES AND ILLNESSES, COW ANATOMY, DINOSAUR MOVEMENT AND VISION, SOFT-TISSUE PRESERVATION, TO EVEN ANCIENT HUMAN CULTURAL INTERACTIONS WITH FOSSILS. YET THE MAJORITY, AND CARY'S AREA OF SPECIALIZATION, ARE DEDICATED TO SAUROPOD DINOSAURS. FROM UNDERSTANDING THEIR GROWTH, TO THE ANATOMY AND PHYSICS OF THESE TITANS, TO EVEN NAMING NEW SPECIES, CARY'S WORK IS HELPING TO BETTER UNDERSTAND THE LIFE HISTORIES AND EVOLUTIONARY STRATEGIES OF WHAT IS UNQUESTIONABLY AND